To:

~~~~~~~~~~~~~~~~~~~~~~

From:

~~~~~~~~~~~~~~~~~~~~~~

Date:

~~~~~~~~~~~~~~~~~~~~~~

The grass withers and the flowers fall,
but the word of the Lord endures forever.

1 Peter 1:24-25

Published by Christian Art Publishers
PO Box 1599, Vereeniging, 1930, RSA

© 2016
First edition 2016

Designed by Christian Art Publishers

Images used under license from Shutterstock.com

Printed in China

ISBN 978-1-4321-1563-0
ISBN 978-1-64272-618-3

21 22 23 24 25 26 27 28 29 30 – 35 34 33 32 31 30 29 28 27 26

PROMISES
TO BLESS YOUR
heart

COLORING BOOK

CHRISTIAN ART
PUBLISHERS

THE LORD IS MY Strength AND MY Song

Exodus 15:2

THIS IS THE
DAY THAT
THE LORD
HAS MADE;
LET US
REJOICE.
PSALM 118:24

THE moon & THE stars YOU set in place.

PSALM 8:3

SHE IS
Clothed
WITH
Strength
AND
dignity
AND SHE
laughs
WITHOUT
FEAR OF THE
future

PROVERBS 31:25

GREAT
IS THE
LORD
&
MOST
WORTHY
OF
PRAISE

Psalm 96:4

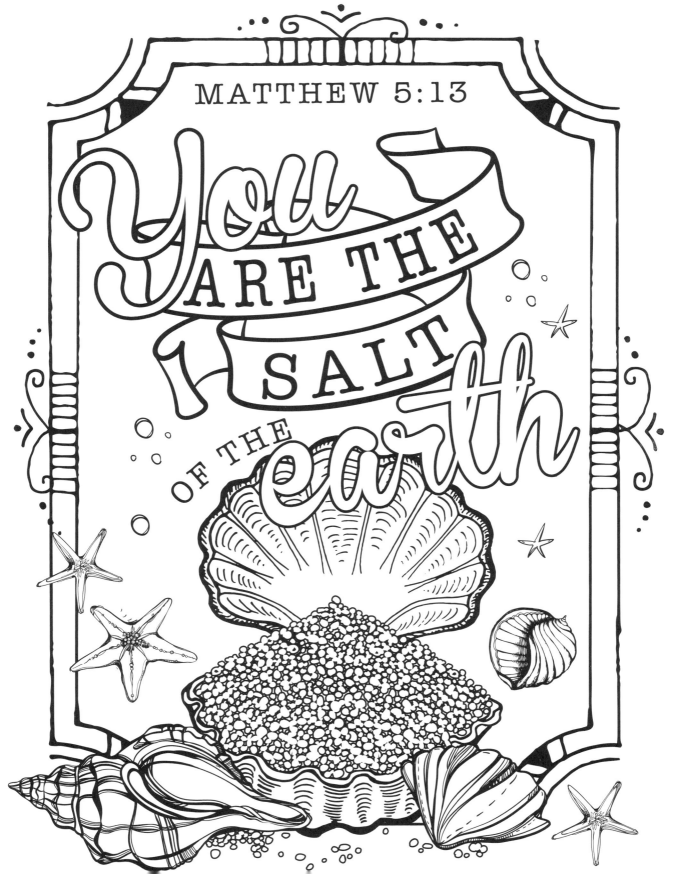

SET YOUR MINDS ON things ABOVE.

COLOSSIANS 3:2

TRUST IN THE LORD WITH ALL YOUR HEART

PROVERBS 3:5

AS FOR ME AND MY

HOUSE

WE WILL SERVE THE LORD.

Joshua 24:15

UNDER HIS WINGS YOU WILL FIND REFUGE

PSALM 91:4

Serve one another in Love

Galatians 5:13

He refreshes my Soul

PSALM 23:3

Clothe yourselves with compassion kindness humility patience gentleness

COLOSSIANS 3:12

THE LORD MY GOD LIGHTS UP MY DARKNESS

PSALM 18:28

EVERY GOOD & PERFECT GIFT IS FROM ABOVE

JAMES 1:17

CALL TO ME

and I will answer you and tell you great and unsearchable things you do not know.

Jeremiah 33:3

His name will be the hope of all the world.

MATTHEW 12:21

HE counts the *Stars* & calls them all by *Name.*

PSALM 147:4

HE WILL cover you with HIS FEATHERS, and under His wings YOU WILL FIND REFUGE.

PSALM 91:4

THE
FAITHFUL
LOVE
OF THE
LORD
NEVER
ENDS
LAMENTATIONS 3:22

FOR IT IS BY GRACE YOU HAVE BEEN SAVED

EPHESIANS 2:8

FOR *everything* THERE IS A *time*

ECCLESIASTES 3:1

MY CUP OVERFLOWS WITH

Blessings

PSALM 23:5

HOPE

FAITH

BOOKMARKS & TAGS
COLOR, CUT, PUNCH AND
TIE A RIBBON

Sing and make music from your heart to the Lord.

Ephesians 5:19

God is with you wherever you go.

Joshua 1:9

"FOR I know the PLANS I HAVE FOR you."

JEREMIAH 29:11

I CAN do ALL things THROUGH Christ WHO STRENGTHENS me.

PHILIPPIANS 4:13

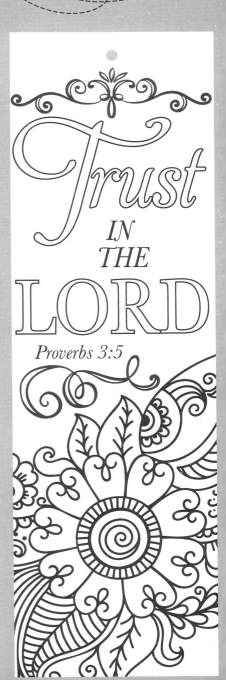

Trust IN THE LORD

Proverbs 3:5

THE LORD WILL
GUIDE YOU ALWAYS.
ISAIAH 58:11

Philippians 4:4

Numbers 6:24

May the Lord
BLESS
you.

Love
NEVER FAILS.
1 CORINTHIANS 13:8

May you be filled
with joy.

Colossians 1:11

BE GLAD IN THE LORD.
PSALM 32:11